CW01150382

Original title:
Crystalline Silences

Copyright © 2024 Creative Arts Management OÜ
All rights reserved.

Author: Evan Hawthorne
ISBN HARDBACK: 978-9916-94-534-6
ISBN PAPERBACK: 978-9916-94-535-3

When Time Stands Still in Silence

In quiet moments, time just snoozes,
Tick-tock sounds are just mere muses.
The clock's confused, it skips a beat,
When all around feels so discreet.

Cotton candy clouds float above,
They laugh and giggle, oh so suave.
The trees tell jokes with rustling leaves,
Nature's stand-up, the best it believes.

Frozen Dance of a Gentle Breeze

A puff of air in a frozen jig,
Waltzing softly, oh what a gig!
It trips on branches, makes leaves swirl,
Like a dancer lost in a twirl.

The daisies nod in quiet glee,
As the breeze throws its little spree.
Whispers of laughter float in space,
Nature's secret, a hidden place.

The Echo of Distant Mountains

Mountains chuckle from way up high,
Their echoes tumble, oh my, oh my!
Like old friends sharing tales of old,
In rumbling laughter, their secrets unfold.

Little critters with ears all perked,
Join the chorus, none feel worked.
They giggle together, plotting their pranks,
Atop those peaks where serenity ranks.

Glimmers of Peace Amidst the Noise

In the clang and clatter, peace resides,
With winks of calm, where chaos hides.
A wink from silence, a gentle peek,
In the maddening buzz, it takes a sneak.

A moment here, a giggle there,
Sparks of joy dance in thin air.
Life's noisy banter, a playful tease,
In the ruckus, find your squeeze of ease.

The Delicate Balance of Light and Quiet

In the hush, where giggles sneak,
Light dances while shadows peek.
A whisper sings, a joke takes flight,
Balancing chuckles, day and night.

The sun winks at the muted breeze,
As ants dance, doing tiny leaps.
A spark ignites, the stillness breaks,
While bread crumbs fall, and laughter wakes.

Shimmering Threads of a Silent Tapestry

In a loom of still, a cat does pounce,
While threads of silence quietly bounce.
The mouse squeaks soft, a clumsy dance,
Life's woven antics make us prance.

Knitting dreams with threads of fun,
Each quiet stitch, a pun begun.
A frayed yarn hangs; we cannot miss,
The comical chaos in tranquil bliss.

An Opalescent Dawn Awakens

Pancakes flip in morning's glow,
While sleepy heads move slow, slow, slow.
The rooster crows with wayward charm,
As socks conspire to cause alarm.

Sunrise giggles wake the trees,
While coffee brews with playful ease.
A spoon does a dance, oh what a sight,
In opalescent rays, we find delight.

The Elsewhere of Quiet Reflections

In puddles deep where voices merge,
Echoes of laughter begin to urge.
A duck quacks loud, a splashy spree,
At the edge of calm, where jokes run free.

Reflections giggle, face to face,
As shadows play a silly chase.
Winks of humor float above,
In this stronghold of chuckles and love.

Echoes of a Shattered Crystal

In a room where laughter sings,
A mirror breaks, oh what a fling!
Reflecting jokes we shouldn't share,
The shards just giggle; who really cares?

A sparkly mess, let's dance around,
Each piece a chuckle, on the ground.
Whispers tumble, like tumbling dice,
Cracking up in shattered ice.

The Weight of Unspoken Thought

A thought balloon, so heavy and round,
It's wobbly, won't leave the ground.
Carrying secrets like a stubborn mule,
Just waiting for someone to act the fool.

We juggle ideas, a comical scene,
Like clowns at a circus—never serene.
The thoughts eventually burst with glee,
Spilling laughter like confetti, whee!

Radiant Stillness of the Void

In the void where crickets chirp,
Silence laughs, oh what a burp!
Nothing happens, yet I trip and fall,
On blank spaces, I can hear it all.

The stillness sways like a lazy cat,
Cuddled up on a floppy mat.
Inside the quiet, giggles boom,
Echoing gently in the gloom.

Fleeting Glimmers of Serenity

A fleeting thought like a soap bubble,
Popped by a laugh, oh what a trouble!
It sparkles bright, then fades to gray,
Tickling cheeks in a silly way.

In moments of peace, we find the jest,
Serenity's cousin—it's all a test.
Chasing glimmers like kids at play,
Giggling softly, come what may.

The Stillness that Breathes

In the garden, a gnome takes a nap,
His hat slumped low, not a peep, just a flap.
The birds laugh loud at his middle-of-day snooze,
While squirrels trade secrets, no chance to refuse.

Underneath the tree, the shadows conspire,
To lure in the cat, who dreams of the fire.
She bounces in silence, paws soft as a kiss,
Chasing dust motes like they're pieces of bliss.

Lost in the Lull of Evening Light

As the sun dips low, toast starts to dance,
Crispy and golden, inviting the chance.
Jam jars are winking, a sweet, sticky sight,
While toast takes a bow, feeling bold and bright.

Beneath flickering stars, the whispers take flight,
A nearby dog howls, claiming his right.
The moon needs a laugh, so it joins the spree,
As fireflies flicker like tiny confetti.

Shadows of Light in the Whispering Wood

In a forest so quiet, the mushrooms convene,
Their caps in a huddle, the gossip unseen.
A deer takes a peek, tiptoes with glee,
Wondering if they're plotting a party for three.

Tall trees stretch their limbs in a slow, silly dance,
Branches doing cha-cha, they're lost in a trance.
The breeze cracks a joke and the leaves start to shake,
As the wood chuckles softly, 'We'll keep you awake.'

Fragments of Memory Suspended in Air

Balloons float by with a giggle and grin,
Each one a dream of the silly within.
They bounce off each other, exchanging a jest,
While kids chase their tails, never needing a rest.

In the clouds, cotton candy starts to melt,
The sun, in its laughter, feels truly felt.
A hiccup from laughter escapes the bright sky,
As shadows curl up, and the echoes fly high.

The Breath of Silent Stones

In corners where whispers dwell,
The stones giggle, what a spell!
They chuckle softly, can't you hear?
Making jokes to the shy deer.

Moss-covered laughter, a soft refrain,
While squirrels tease, 'Are you insane?'
With every creak and every crack,
The earth snickers, never slack.

Ethereal Clarity

Oh, the air's so clear today,
Like a ghost in a ballet!
It tickles noses, makes us sneeze,
While clouds form shapes like jelly peas.

The sun beams down with silly grace,
As shadows dance and take their place.
The breeze shouts jokes, we laugh aloud,
In this clear space, we're all so proud.

Frost-Flecked Tranquility

Frosty patterns, a chilly tease,
On windows, they giggle like fairies, please!
Whispering secrets in shiny hues,
While we sip cocoa, sharing our views.

The world outside is a prankster's scheme,
With icicles laughing, like they're a dream.
As snowflakes twirl, they mischief prance,
In this frosty laughter, we all dance.

A Dance of Cold Air

The cold air shimmies with a twist,
Tickling cheeks, a frosty mist.
It teases the trees to shake off their leaves,
While robins strut in their winter weaves.

With playful gusts, the hats take flight,
Chasing each other in sheer delight.
The world spins round in a crisp embrace,
As we join in this absurd race.

The Geometry of Quiet Moments

In corners where whispers lay,
A triangle forms, in odd array.
It tickles ears with secret jokes,
As shadows dance like frosty folks.

The square in silence, plotting glee,
Is lacking sides, but full of spree.
The hypotenuse winks, what a tease,
As giggles float like gentle breeze.

A Mirage of Glacial Resonance

In frigid air, a chuckle flows,
While snowflakes blush with timid pose.
They slip and slide, then burst with cheer,
Creating symphonies from cold sphere.

The icicles hum a playful tune,
As frosty critters croon in June.
A polar bear, with witty flair,
Joins in the mirth, he's quite the pair.

Light's Veil of Serenity

Behind the curtain of soft beams,
A droll shadow stirs, or so it seems.
It jiggles through, with playful zeal,
A luminous prank, can you feel?

The glow appears, a jester bold,
With giggles wrapped in warmth untold.
As dawn peeks in, it starts to play,
In light's embrace, we dance and sway.

The Calm Before Shimmering Dawn

Right before the world awakes,
A kooky silence, silence shakes.
The moon winks down with knowing laugh,
While stars conspire on a fun path.

The breeze conspires with the night,
In breezy talks, they share delight.
A yawning sun prepares to rise,
And soon erupts with bright surprise.

Secrets Held in Stillness

In corners where the echoes play,
A cat naps, dreaming of ballet.
Secrets hide beneath the fluff,
Whispers giggle—it's all quite tough.

A dust mote twirls like a twirling dancer,
While the dog plots its next great prancer.
Socks vanish as if in a trance,
Leaving humanity in a sockless dance.

Hushed tones tumble from the ceiling,
The bowl of popcorn, now revealing:
Crisp kernels burst with laughter bright,
As midnight snacks take graceful flight.

So gather 'round in muted glee,
Where silence sings, and you might see,
The joy that lives in stillness' charm,
A world of giggles, soft and warm.

Hidden Luminescence

Beneath the couch, a glow so sly,
Is mom's lost phone, oh me, oh my!
It lights up like a disco ball,
Inviting all to dance and sprawl.

The fridge hums tunes of forgotten fare,
Lemonade ghosts whispering 'we're rare!'
In the cereal box, a party's aglow,
With marshmallow guest, 'Do you want to know?'

The showerhead sings in harmony,
As soap bubbles float like a symphony.
Toilet paper rolls break into song,
Preparing for laughs, the night won't be long.

In closets, socks frolic unkempt,
Creating a world where laughter's exempt.
So embrace the glow in hidden spots,
Where silliness lives in quirky knots.

Voices Wrapped in Dew

In morning's blush, the grass takes a bow,
Bees hold a meeting—oh, who knew how?
A leaf shivers, calls out 'Morning cheer!'
While dewdrops giggle without any fear.

Ants in a line host a tiny parade,
With crumbs as confetti—hooray, hooray!
They march to their tune, a hum, and a buzz,
Unraveling tales as only ants would.

A pigeon coos gossip from the park bench,
While squirrels exchange nuts in a wild wrench.
The sun peeks in, nodding with grace,
As laughter flutters in the cool air's embrace.

So take a stroll where the whispers twine,
And listen closely, the tales—divine!
In realms of dew where joy does flow,
Nature's jesters put on a show.

Luminescent Whispers

Overhead, the twinkling stars play tricks,
While raccoons plot mischief with all their picks.
Shiny objects caught in their sights,
Hold the stories of magical nights.

In the moon's glow, the owls convene,
To share their secrets, playful and keen.
With every hoot, a cosmic jest,
Making the night feel truly blessed.

The fireflies blink codes of delight,
Sparking laughter in the stillness of night.
And the trees sway, with chuckling leaves,
Creating a symphony that never deceives.

Beneath the stars, the world in giggles,
Whispers of night playfully wiggles.
So dance with the glow, let the laughter beam,
In echoes of joy, let your spirit dream.

Moments Wrapped in Ice

A penguin slips and does a spin,
Snowballs fly, it's time to grin!
Frosty nose and chilly toes,
Winter fun in frozen throws.

Icicles hang like toothy grins,
Snowmen dance while the cold wind spins.
With mittens thick and laughter loud,
We twirl and shout, we feel so proud.

Hot cocoa waits, all marshmallowy,
But first we have to build a teepee.
In frosty air, with hearts so light,
We giggle 'til we say goodnight.

Now the moon starts to shine so bright,
As stars appear in winter's night.
With snowy plumage all around,
We find the joy where cold is found.

Dancers in the Still Twilight

In twilight's glow, the shadows play,
Snowflakes twirl, they steal the day.
With twinkling lights and frosty breath,
We dance around, defying death.

A rabbit hops, a little shy,
It joins the jive with a joyful sigh.
As fireflies wink, there's magic afoot,
Nature's chorus, we all salute.

The stars are shy but peek out wide,
While frozen branches dance with pride.
With every step, we spin and glide,
Around the path of the snowy slide.

Laughter rings through the winter air,
With friends and fun beyond compare.
At dawn's first light, we'll call it peace,
But first, let's dance, let laughter increase!

Veils of Mist on Still Ponds

Ponds reflect the frosty veil,
While ducks parade, they never fail.
With wobbly feet, they slip and slide,
Mist cloaks them, oh what a ride!

In the quiet, whispers sing,
Frogs croak loudly, the mist is king.
We toss snow in playful glee,
Watch it settle, a fun debris.

A hermit crab in shades of blue,
Joins the dance, it's such a zoo!
Each splash tells tales, with silly grace,
As laughter bounces in this place.

In these moments, joy we seek,
With playful pranks, we seldom peek.
As dawn unfolds the misty shrouds,
We wave goodbye to winter crowds.

Frozen Frames of Eternal Peace

Snapshots caught in icy grasp,
Moments frozen in a laugh, a gasp.
A polar bear in furs of white,
Practices its dance in soft moonlight.

With cheeks so rosy, we sit and play,
Snowflake soccer, what a day!
Giggles echo in the cold,
We swap our tales of brave and bold.

Hot soup bubbles on frosty stoves,
While kittens pounce in all their loves.
With every bite, we warm our hearts,
And share the joy of frozen arts.

As twilight falls, we snuggle tight,
In blankets wrapped, all cozy and bright.
Each frozen frame a cherished tease,
Forever kept in winter's breeze.

The Quiet Dance of Shimmering Light

In a room where echoes play,
The dust bunnies dance away.
A mischievous wink from the dawn,
Whispers of morning fun are born.

Lampshades wiggle, curtains sway,
While mice put on a grand ballet.
A gleam of moonlight strikes a pose,
Ready for the night's grand shows.

Chandeliers giggle with delight,
As shadows twirl in soft moonlight.
The clock takes a very long pause,
While the floorboards break into applause.

The silent chorus hums a tune,
As chairs waltz beneath the moon.
Every creak a cheerful sound,
Where silliness knows no bound.

Ethereal Reflections in Still Waters

Upon the pond a frog does leap,
Making waves that softly peep.
A ripple sparkles, like a wink,
While fish below begin to think.

The lily pads are wearing hats,
And hosting debates with polite chats.
A dragonfly dons a sleek tie,
While cattails sway and flutter by.

Reflections twist in giggling glee,
A mirror where they want to be.
Nymphs in the reeds share secrets,
As laughter sprouts from hidden niches.

The stillness hums a funny tune,
As frogs croon 'Underneath the Moon'.
Pond life dances, a joyful show,
In the waters, embarrassment's low.

Glassy Fragments of Forgotten Dreams

In a cupboard, the glassware sighs,
As memories sparkle in their eyes.
A cracked mug laughs at its own fate,
While plates spin tales of culinary hate.

The shattered fragments stow away,
In shadows where forgotten dreams play.
Each shard reflects a silly grin,
Recalling moments buried within.

A china cat rolls with a paw,
And nicks the chips in whimsical awe.
Each crack a laugh, a tale to tell,
In the attic where the dust bunnies dwell.

Among the fragments, jesters cheer,
Recalling every autumn beer.
In this chaos, joy weaves its seam,
In glassy parts of a dreamy theme.

Shadows Cast by Tranquil Minds

In corners where the shadows dance,
Ideas twirl in a funny trance.
A fleeting thought takes light to roam,
While echoes giggle of the unknown.

The quiet mind is a playful jest,
Making shadows work their best.
Hiding secrets, whispering well,
As the sun bids the night to swell.

Ideas swirl like paper planes,
Sailing softly on the brain trains.
Every shadow, a thoughtful laugh,
Sketching whims on a mental path.

The twilight sparks a playful chase,
As silliness fills this mental space.
In tranquil moments where shadows gleam,
The laughter brews within the dream.

Whispers of Ice

In a frosty breeze, giggles fly,
Ice cubes clink, oh my, oh my!
Snowflakes dance with a cheeky flair,
Laughing softly, filling the air.

Penguins waddle, wearing a grin,
Chasing dreams on a frozen whim.
Their little tuxedos, perfectly neat,
Slipping and sliding on chilly street.

Icicles dangle like quirky glints,
Mischief sparkles in every hint.
Frosty friends in frolic abound,
Making memories without a sound.

Snowmen chat with noses so bright,
Hats askew, what a silly sight!
Dress them up and watch them sway,
In the winter's chilly play.

Glistening Stillness

A glittering hush drapes the lane,
Where frosty flakes fall like champagne.
Laughter echoes, a chilly spree,
As ice skates twirl so joyfully.

Subtle whispers of snowflakes fall,
Like secrets traded by one and all.
Bouncing snowballs drum beats so light,
A snowy meeting, what a delight!

Chill in the air, but spirits high,
Sledding down hills with a joyful sigh.
Hot cocoa waits at the cabin door,
To warm our hearts for even more.

Frosty fingers play jolly tunes,
As snowmen burst into silly croons.
With every laugh, the stillness breaks,
In a world where joy and fun awakes.

Echoes in Frost

In the quiet dusk, a tickle is heard,
The soft hum of winter, a playful bird.
Sipping on cocoa with marshmallows bright,
Even the stars giggle in the night.

The frost on windows, a sparkling disguise,
Where laughter lingers and no one cries.
They sketch a dance of patterns so fine,
As giggles mingle with sweet, warm wine.

Footprints crunch on the frosty ground,
The merry echoes of joy abound.
Bulging snowballs tossed in delight,
While frost and humor unite in the night.

Children play, with cheeks rosy and red,
Telling tall tales of snowflakes, they said.
In every giggle, the magic is found,
In winter's embrace, where joy knows no bounds.

The Hush of Transparent Dreams

Under the moon, where silence gleams,
Laughter floats on translucent beams.
Snowflakes shimmer with mischievous glee,
Whispering secrets for all to see.

Frosty windows draw whimsical sights,
Teenage snowmen planning wild nights!
They sport sunglasses, in all their flair,
Plotting a winter parade with care.

Fluffy clouds hosting a giggle fest,
Angels chuckling in snow-woven vests.
With each gentle flutter, the stillness breaks,
In the hush of the dream where every heart quakes.

Lacing boots for a frosty race,
Each stumble and slip, a laugh to embrace.
Frosted laughter, a dance so grand,
In the quiet dreams we all understand.

The Serenity of Shattered Light

In the land of broken beams,
Laughter bounces off the walls.
A chandelier's dance with dust,
Breaks the quiet with its calls.

Sunbeams waltz on shattered glass,
Giggles slip through every crack.
The sunlight's teasing, oh so bold,
As it sends shadows on a track.

A prism writes a chaotic tale,
Where silly rainbows burst outside.
Each hue a joke, a color's laugh,
In this light show, let's abide.

Laughter echoes in strange tones,
In the silence, light can play.
So let's sip our shattered dreams,
And giggle our blues away.

Moments Suspended in Time

Tick tock goes the clock's bold wink,
Time trips over shoelaces tight.
Frozen poses, smiles that blink,
As seconds stop, the world gets light.

Each minute hangs like a ripe fruit,
Daring us to pluck its cheer.
Yet here we are, wrapped in a suit,
Of moments paused, let's draw near.

A snapshot of giggles painted bright,
Where laughter holds a joking breath.
Time can tumble in delight,
Finding joy in its own death.

Let's transform clocks with silly games,
And skip the hours, dance 'til noon.
For life's too funny for dry claims,
Let's laugh beneath this silly moon.

Echoes of Tranquil Landscapes

In the field of whispers, jokes collide,
As daisies snicker, tickling their roots.
The trees are jesters, with arms open wide,
Concealing giggles in leafy suits.

Mountains chuckle with their grand looks,
While rivers gurgle with a sly wink.
Nature's humor, nestled in books,
Whispers warmth in every clink.

A boulder grins beneath the sky,
In its stillness tales unfold.
Blades of grass sway, asking why,
And weaving in chuckles untold.

The echoes of calm hold laughter's spark,
In each serene step, the jokes are bright.
As landscapes shout in whispers dark,
They say, "Relax, it's all alright!"

Spheres of Serenity under the Moon

Under the orb that likes to grin,
Spheres of nonsense roll around.
Moonbeams stretch, inviting in,
A giggle that dances, not a sound.

Frogs croon ballads of wild delight,
To the serenade of starry plights.
In the moon's glow, everything feels light,
As shadows play, taking playful flights.

Marshmallows float in the night air high,
Chasing dreams with each silly leap.
While night's silence can't help but sigh,
In this hush, laughter takes a sweep.

So come my friend, let's roam around,
In this sphere where fun runs free.
Beneath the moon's watchful eyes,
Let's laugh until we can't see!

The Glint of Stars in Midnight Silence

In the night, stars play peek-a-boo,
Twinkling winks, just for me and you.
They giggle softly, shining bright,
A cosmic joke in the still of night.

Moonbeams dance like kittens at play,
Laughing around, never shy nor gray.
A comet zips by, a silly face,
In this quiet, we find a pace.

Each star's a wink, each wink a cheer,
Gathering laughter, spreading good cheer.
In a universe vast, we're all in on it,
A shared chuckle in the moonlit skit.

Beneath this wink, worries take a dive,
In the humor of night, we come alive.
Laughter rises, light as the breeze,
In the stillness, we find our ease.

Still Waters Reflecting Dreams

A pond that giggles under the sun,
Mirrors dreams, but it's just for fun.
The frogs croak jokes, silly and loud,
While fish flip stories, oh so proud.

Ripples of laughter, quick as a dart,
Splashing reflections, a comical art.
Each wave a chuckle, each droplet sings,
Of midnight snacks and silly flings.

Ducklings parade with a swaggering strut,
Quacking like comedians, oh what a rut.
With every splash, joy takes its flight,
The water chuckles into the night.

Quiet and playful, the surface shall gleam,
A canvas of humor, a whimsical theme.
Time drips slowly, like honey, it seems,
Beneath this stillness, there's laughter in dreams.

Whispers Amidst Glistening Leaves

Leaves have secrets hidden from view,
Murmuring tales of the old and the new.
Branches wobble, a timeless jest,
Frogs on the sidelines, taking a rest.

Laughter rustles through the green so bright,
Tickling the air with pure delight.
In the breeze, whispers weave a tale,
Of squirrels who trip and nincompoops who fail.

Sunlight dapples, casting shadows fun,
Dancing with mischief, they frolic and run.
Every rustle, a giggle in disguise,
In this leafy laughter, joy surely lies.

Nature's jesters, at work and play,
Mixing the mundane with the gay.
Among the leaves that shimmer and sway,
Whispers of humor brighten the day.

Frozen Conversations with the Moon

Under stars, the moon takes a seat,
Cracks a joke, isn't that neat?
In frozen stillness, thoughts collide,
With lighthearted banter, the universe wide.

Snowflakes giggle, falling in grace,
As moonlight whispers, "Let's pick up the pace!"
With frozen smiles, they sway and mold,
While the world below shivers and folds.

Stars snicker softly at secrets untold,
Frosted confessions, brave and bold.
Every glimmer, a punchline to share,
In frozen moments, humor fills the air.

So dance in the moonlight, let laughter bloom,
In the stillness, there's always room.
For cosmic chuckles, under the sky,
With frozen conversations, we laugh and fly.

Hushed Symphony of Ice

In winter's grip, the silence plays,
A tune of whispers, soft displays.
Snowflakes dance in flurry, so bright,
Tickling noses, pure delight.

The icicles hang like frozen cheer,
Now look, there's one—oh dear, oh dear!
It fell on me like a sneaky ninja,
I swear it laughed, the icy fringe-a!

In this frosty world, we almost slide,
Like clowns on ice, with pride denied.
Yet giggles melt in frosty air,
As snowmen grin, without a care.

So let us toast with hot cocoa bliss,
To frozen shenanigans, can't let them miss!
A symphony of laughter in the cold,
The best ice age story ever told.

The Stillness Between Thoughts

Thoughts freeze like puddles in the sun,
Waiting for warmth, oh what a pun!
We giggle as we ponder, then break,
In a land where ideas are hard to shake.

In the quiet, a tingle stirs,
Beneath the calm, mischief purrs.
A brain freeze has never been so fun,
As ideas play tag, and we all run!

Like popcorn kernels, ready to pop,
Introspection may cause a mental flop.
But hey, at least we can sit and smile,
In the stillness, let's ponder for a while.

Each pause bounces in a wobbly way,
Thoughts like ice cubes in a cocktail play.
Oh, the silliness hiding in all the quiet,
Isn't that where we find the riot!

A Fractured Glass Serenity

In shards of humor, laughter gleams,
Like broken mirrors reflecting dreams.
A little crack, a little light,
Turns chaos into comic delight.

Whispers bounce off shattered glass,
Each one's a joke, a winking pass.
The world spins 'round like a disco ball,
Where all our giggles suddenly sprawl.

So trip a little, oh don't you dare,
To shatter the silence with a buffoon's flair!
With every tumble and clumsy dance,
A playful chuckle becomes the chance.

Let's gather these shards into a vase,
A jester's crown in our silly chase.
In every crack, a story resides,
In fractured beauty, humor abides.

Murmurs Beneath Frozen Leaves

Beneath the frost, a giggle hides,
Among the leaves, the secret slides.
Squirrels gossip with winter's chill,
Caching nuts for the silly thrill.

Each whisper rustles like a joke,
Leaves tremble at every poke.
Nature's chuckle in snow's embrace,
As winter winks at the frosty place.

The ice all giggles—can you hear?
It's a comedy show that's sure to clear.
With every flake that falls today,
The world's a stage for the frosty play.

So let's dive deep, beneath the white,
And join the murmurs, to twist and write.
In chilly breezes, we find our lore,
Where leaves giggle and whisper, "More!"

Stillness Carved in Time

In a world where time stands still,
Penguins play with frigid will.
Snowmen dance in frozen bliss,
While icicles share a frosty kiss.

A squirrel slides on icy slopes,
Chasing dreams with silly hopes.
The sun chuckles, it's a sight,
As shadows twirl in pure delight.

Chattering skates on glassy lakes,
Popcorn clouds, no room for breaks.
Winter's jesters, here they come,
Spreading cheer, a frosty hum.

Even the breath of chilly air,
Has jokes to share, so light and rare.
In this stillness, laughter thrives,
In frozen moments, playfulness drives.

Reflections of a Frozen Heart

When the mirror freezes bright,
Reflections giggle with delight.
A snowflake winks as it swirls by,
With dreams of flying high in the sky.

A heart encased in icy lace,
Thinks of love, then makes a face.
It flutters, cracks, a funny sight,
As warmth creeps in to chase the night.

Pine cones gossip with the breeze,
Whispering secrets to the trees.
As frosty laughter fills the air,
Even the rabbits stop to stare.

With every freeze, a joke is spun,
In chilly realms, there's lots of fun.
A stillness here, but don't despair,
For frozen hearts can still declare.

Whispers of Frozen Echoes

Echoes bounce on icy trails,
Telling tales of silly gales.
Snowflakes giggle as they fall,
A surprise party for one and all.

The trees sway gently, a mock ballet,
While frostbitten squirrels sneak away.
They grab a snack, a daring feat,
And trip on snow with wobbly feet.

In this world where cold prevails,
Each sound is wrapped in sparkling veils.
Laughing spirits swirl around,
Crafting joy without a sound.

So heed the whispers in the chill,
Each frozen note brings laughter still.
Here in this land of winter's cheer,
Echoes of joy are always near.

Luminous Echoes at Dawn

Dawn breaks with a smile so bright,
Painting snow in golden light.
Frosty air dares to proclaim,
That winter's dance is not so tame.

Crystalline bubbles, laughter soars,
As sunlight knocks on frozen doors.
The penguins shiver, they can't resist,
And join the jig with frosty twists.

Each step on ice is a daring game,
As giggles echo without shame.
The sun winks at the winter's show,
Sprinkling sparkles, stealing the glow.

In this mirthful morning glow,
Nature shares her funny show.
With every laugh, the day begins,
In this wondrous land where joy wins.

Silential Harmonies of Nature's Breath

In the woods where whispers start,
Squirrels gossip, oh so smart.
Leaves giggle in the breeze,
Nature sings with playful ease.

Bees hum tunes of secret cheer,
Tiny ants dance, never fear.
In the hush, a rabbit grins,
As he wins the hide-and-seek spins.

Mossy carpets, they gleam with glee,
A snail slips by with careful decree.
Frogs croak laughs, a funny toad,
As nature's jesters share the road.

Silent echoes burst with sound,
In this world, pure joy is found.
Nature's laughter, soft yet bright,
Filling hearts with sheer delight.

The Glistening Veil of Quietude

Morning dew starts the day,
Whispers weave in a playful way.
The sun peeks through with a wink,
Grass blades sway, they're in sync.

A sleepy cat on the fence,
Prowls the world, it's so suspense!
She pounces at shadows in sight,
Turns out it's just a leaf in flight.

Clouds drift slowly, having fun,
Playing tag with the bright sun.
A parrot squawks, a jokester proud,
As the sky wears a fluffy cloud.

Nature chuckles, her secrets bloom,
In quietude, there's no room for gloom.
Every sound, a twist or tease,
In this stillness, joy comes with ease.

Frozen Verses Beneath a Starry Sky

Starry nights, a canvas wide,
Owls and crickets, side by side.
They share tales in whispered tones,
Under the moon, they call their own.

A raccoon, masked and full of flair,
Jumps and jests without a care.
Slipping on ice, oh what a sight,
Even the stars giggle with delight!

Frosty grasses twinkle and gleam,
Nature's sparkle, like a dream.
As fireflies flicker, play and tease,
Nighttime mischief puts minds at ease.

Beneath twinkling lights, soft and shy,
The constellations seem to fly.
In every pause, a laugh we find,
Under a quilt of night, so kind.

Luminescent Dreams in the Stillness

As moonbeams dance on the lake,
Frogs orchestrate a grand mistake.
One jumps high, then lands with a plop,
Their ribbits echo, then come to a stop.

Fireflies glimmer, like stars on cue,
Chasing shadows, a silly debut.
A bumblebee's buzz, so light and brief,
Spins around like it's chasing a thief.

Crickets chirp a comedic tune,
Swapping stories under the moon.
A raccoon sneaks with a pie in paw,
Caught mid-caper, it's quite the draw!

In this stillness, laughter reigns,
Dreams sparkle like the midnight trains.
Nature's humor, forever bold,
In her quiet, funny tales unfold.

Hibernating Voices Beneath Frost

In the blanket of white, they doze,
Whispers of dreams that nobody knows.
Squirrels in winter pajamas collide,
Sneaking snacks with a giggling pride.

Frogs sing lullabies, oh so sweet,
While fish spin tales on tiny, cold feet.
Snowflakes fall with a flick of a wrist,
Even the owls can't resist the twist.

Bears in their dens, snoring in tune,
Hoping for snacks, like salad and prunes.
Frosty air tickles, makes noses twitch,
Wintertime antics, without a hitch.

Tails wrapped like presents, snug and round,
Chasing each other in soft snow mound.
A ruckus unfolds with every snap,
Winter's comedy, a cozy mishap.

Unspoken Songs of Tranquil Waters

Ripples dance where the fish hold sway,
Giggling bubbles come out to play.
Here, frogs croak their secret refrain,
Water leaves with no hint of pain.

With a splash and a kick, the ducks take flight,
Waddling humor, a comical sight.
They quack of adventures, lost in the reeds,
Singing of breadcrumbs, their fanciful needs.

Murmurs of waters, tantalizing tease,
Tickling some catfish, down on their knees.
The dragonflies dance in a playful spin,
Creating a ruckus where troubles begin.

Beneath the calm, the laughter ignites,
Unseen, unsung, in aquatic delights.
The pond holds secrets, giggles abound,
In unspoken songs, hilariously found.

Glassy Wings of the Morning Light

Butterflies twirl in the sun's soft kiss,
Chasing each other, oh, what a bliss!
Their antics in flight are a sight you can't miss,
As dragonflies laugh in a dew-drenched twist.

Light filters through leaves with a shimmering gleam,
Birds try to whistle, but it's more like a meme.
A jumbled cacophony, happy and bright,
Nature's own chorus, a morning delight.

The sun winks down on the flowers so fair,
While honeybees stumble, lost in their flair.
Nectar's their bourbon, they dance with such zeal,
Life's too short to just hover and peel.

Wings of glass shimmer, in a humorous game,
Chasing the sunshine, it's never the same.
Each flutter and flap brings a chuckle so loud,
In the morning light, laughter's proud.

The Breathe of Quiet Waters

Streams softly chuckle, secrets they share,
Ripples of laughter hang in the air.
The stones on the bed hum a gentle tune,
While tadpoles wiggle beneath the bright moon.

Mosses gossip, so green and so bright,
Telling of frogs who boast of their height.
A splash from a turtle, how daring a feat,
Each ripple igniting a giggling beat.

Drifting on currents, the lilies play hide,
As frogs leap for glory with leaps full of pride.
The breeze joins in, tickling the grass,
Nature's orchestra, no moment to pass.

Quiet waters laugh in their own playful way,
Sharing their stories of night and of day.
With humor and whispers, the world feels alive,
In the breathe of the waters, joy will thrive.

Still Waters Reflecting Light

In the pond, fish strike a pose,
Like they're coy models, perfect and prose.
Splashing around, they think they're so slick,
But their dance is just a clumsy trick.

The frogs leap in, shouting with glee,
Claiming the surface as their own spree.
With a croak and a plop, they make quite the scene,
Splashing the stillness, oh what a routine!

Reflections quiver, giggles arise,
As geese parade, adorned with surprise.
They strut like royalty, flapping their wings,
Adding chaos to calm, it's a riot of things!

But the water just chuckles, keeps all its charms,
While critters create their own funny alarms.
In this peaceful realm of light and delight,
Life's a funny ballet, from morning till night.

Secrets in a Fragile Glaze

A shard of glass, a secret untold,
Reflects the past where adventures unfold.
Tiny whispers of jokes in the breeze,
Caught in the magic of giggling trees.

The moon sneaks in, winks with a grin,
As the stars watch closely, their mischief begins.
They twinkle and tease, like kids in a game,
Creating a ruckus without any blame.

Butterflies flutter with colorful flair,
Playing tag with the wind, without a care.
Each secret they carry, a gift made of light,
In fragile reflections, they take their flight.

The glassy surface, a mirror of jest,
Captures the laughter, puts joy to the test.
In this whimsy of shadows, the world sings a tune,
Secrets of joy, as bright as the moon.

A Tapestry of Shimmering Calm

Waves of laughter stitch together the night,
As the stars trade their secrets, oh what a sight!
A tapestry woven with giggles and dreams,
Under the veil of moonlight's soft beams.

Each ripple a smile, each splash a delight,
Fishes tell stories of bold, silly fright.
Turtles in hats tiptoe on their toes,
Creating a ruckus wherever they go!

Reflecting their antics, the water claps back,
With bubbles that burst in a comical track.
The calm doesn't mind, it knows all the fun,
In this strange little world, life's a pun under the sun.

Even the crickets join in the mirth,
Chirping out jokes, sharing their worth.
In this shimmering blend of laughter and light,
A tapestry glimmers, oh, what a night!

Shadows on a Glassy Surface

Beneath the glass, shadows laugh and play,
Tiptoe and tumble in their own wacky way.
They stretch and they yawn, like a cat in the sun,
Creating a spectacle, oh what fun!

Glimmers of silliness dance all around,
As the sun's golden rays tickle the ground.
The ducks are the stars, in a comical role,
Diving and splashing, they steal the whole show.

Each ripple creates an exciting cascade,
Of giggles and whispers where troubles just fade.
The surface might shimmer, but oh, what a scene,
Life's funny ballet, both silly and serene!

So here's to the shadows, the laughter they spread,
In this watery world where joy is widespread.
On a glassy canvas, let's paint with delight,
For life's all about finding the funny in sight.

Shards of Quiet Reflection

In the still of the night, pigeons coo loud,
They tiptoe on ice with a waddling crowd.
Glimmers of silence hang thick in the air,
While squirrels in snow gear plot without care.

The snowflakes dance like they've lost their way,
Chasing each other like kids at play.
A yawn from a bear, what a sight to behold,
While penguins argue over who's less cold.

The trees wear their coats, a sparkling sheen,
Discussing the weather like they're quite keen.
A tickle of laughter escapes from a seam,
While the moon rolls its eyes at the daytime dream.

In pockets of laughter, the quiet takes flight,
With giggles from shadows that squabble at night.
Snowmen whisper secrets, their noses askew,
And the stars, oh so sassy, wear frosty dew.

Murmurs Beneath the Ice

Bubbles of laughter float under the freeze,
While fish tell tall tales that bring people to ease.
The pond's little whispers become quite a feast,
As frogs join to croak out a risqué little beast.

The ice, like a stage, plays host to the show,
As otters glide by on a brightening flow.
They juggle their fish with a flick and a flair,
While the turtles politely pretend not to care.

There's a walrus who hums a bizarre little tune,
Claiming it brings forth a lovely buffoon.
While seagulls dive down for a whirl in the fun,
It's a full-blown soirée under the warm sun.

From beneath, a chorus of chuckles arise,
Ghostly shadows scatter with glinting surprise.
With each little giggle that makes bodies sway,
The icy façade shrinks; it's a wild cabaret.

Luminous Solitude

Alone in the glow, a light bulb's bright thought,
It yearns for a buddy, but all it has wrought,
Are cobwebs of dreams and a dust bunny thief,
In the corners of quiet, there's no disbelief.

The walls, they confide in a creak and a sigh,
Echoing chuckles as time passes by.
The fridge holds the gossip of leftovers true,
While a cat devises its plot for a coup.

A chair softly squeaks like it knows all the jokes,
While lampshades decide to join in the pokes,
And a mouse taps its foot to the rhythm of dust,
As the clock ticks in tempo, it's all just for us.

In the heart of the night, the silence will hum,
With echoes of lunacy, it becomes quite fun.
For in every single flicker, you'll find a delight,
In luminous moments where all feels just right.

The Sound of Frosted Space

In the hush of the frost, where whispering beams,
Create tales of mischief and whimsical dreams.
The wind's a composer of notes soft and spry,
While snowflakes indulge in their own waltz to fly.

Beneath all the layers, the giggles are grand,
Where icicles dangle like a mischievous band.
Each drip of the thaw is a tip-toeing joke,
As the frost takes a bow, the tickles provoke.

In fluffy white clouds, the secrets grow bold,
While deer in their coats strut, a sight to behold.
They prance in the moonlight, all frosty and bright,
With humor infused in the stillness of night.

And nature, it chuckles with all of its might,
Each shimmer of snow is a pause for delight.
For in this vast silence, where witticisms race,
Lives the joy of the merry in frosted space.

The Frosted Silence of Winter Nights

Snowflakes dance like tiny jesters,
Hiding giggles in the frost.
The moon's a wink, it's playtime too,
While chilly winds wonder who's lost.

Squirrels toss snowballs on the run,
Their laughter echoes through the pines.
A thermal snicker from the sun,
As it peeks through wintery lines.

Carrots in noses, hats askew,
Frosty friends just want to play.
Wrapped in scarves, they trip and stew,
In a snowball fight's classic way.

Bundled up, they share a cheer,
Each slip an opera full of glee.
Winter's magic, sweet and clear,
In frosty silence, joyful spree.

Shards of Clarity in the Quiet

Amidst shadows, giggles break,
Each sound a diamond in disguise.
Jokes trapped in the light of day,
Revealed when laughter sets the skies.

Echoes slide on glassy beams,
Frogs wear ties for their grand dance.
In moonlit dreams, the silliness seems,
Like kittens dressed in polka pants.

Whispers bounce on airy wings,
As tree branches play hide and seek.
Even the stars, in twinkling rings,
Join in the fun—a cosmic cheek!

What is this joy that fills the night?
A riddle spun from silver strands.
Each chuckle makes the dark feel bright,
In the stillness, oddity stands.

Twinkling Whispers of Distant Stars

In the night, they wink and tease,
Stars beam jokes from far away.
Their laughter drifts on cosmic breeze,
To tickle hearts in grand array.

Comets race with tails of cheer,
Shooting through as the moons combine.
Galaxies giggle, oh so near,
Painting skies with a cheeky line.

Planets roll like mischievous sprites,
Spinning tales of wonder and jest.
A dance of light ignites the nights,
In the universe's playful quest.

Why do they laugh? Who knows the cause!
Perhaps a cosmic sense of fun.
In this vastness, each spark applause,
Creating magic as day is done.

Silent Gleam Amidst the Shadows

In the dark, giggles softly flow,
Each shimmer hides a playful grin.
The shadows chuckle, don't they know?
Their frolics spark where dreams begin.

A mischief-maker in the glow,
Whispering secrets none can hear.
The moon rolls eyes, caught in the show,
As stars conspire—oh dear, oh dear!

Lamp posts yawn as crickets sing,
Nighttime jesters spin their tales.
Even the crickets wear a ring,
As laughter floats on velvet sails.

Silence drips with a tinkle bright,
In the corners where shadows loom.
Together they breathe, a joyful sight,
Crafting joy from the quiet's room.

Elysium of Whispered Thoughts

In the land where whispers play,
Quiet thoughts dance on display.
Echoing giggles, a frosty tease,
Tickles the mind with playful ease.

Pondering if snowflakes conspire,
A secret summit, plan for higher.
Chattering clouds in a fluffy jam,
While squirrels debate like a comedy clan.

Each breeze a chuckle, a sneaky grin,
Raindrops fall, they clap, they spin.
In this realm where glee is rife,
Every thought has a comical life.

So tiptoe softly, laugh out loud,
In this whispering, giggling crowd.
Elysium waits for those who seek,
A gentle smile, a loving peek!

The Secret Lives of Icicles

Icicles hang with a pointy flair,
Secret agents with frosty air.
They plot their drift as snowflakes gossip,
Hatching schemes like a winter rocketship.

They glimmer and wink in the crisp bright light,
Conspiring to fall with comedic delight.
'Look at me!' they seem to say,
'Just wait for that unsuspecting day!'

But when the sun smirks, they're on their way,
Melting mischief, gone to play.
A drip, a splash, a sudden thrill,
Oh the tales they tell from the frozen chill!

So tip your hat to those frozen spies,
In their world of laughter beneath winter skies.
Life is a joke, one they knew well,
Icicles wink, and who can tell?

Soft Footfalls on Sparkling Snow

The snow is a canvas, all quiet and bright,
With soft footfalls that dance in light.
Each crunch a giggle, a laugh with flair,
Like secret whispers in frosty air.

Snowmen chuckle with carrot noses,
As children build in their winter poses.
Falling flat, making a snow angel,
The giggles spread like a jolly jangle.

Snowballs fly with a playful snicker,
As laughter echoes, getting thicker.
Each frosty prank, a giggling spree,
Life's silly moments, wild and free.

Soft footfalls lead to whimsical fun,
In a world of snow where jokes are spun.
So join the dance, leave worries behind,
In this winter's laughter, joy you will find!

The Weight of Soft Echoes

Echoes float on a pillow of sound,
Light as feathers, they swirl around.
Each giggle bounces, a soft refrain,
In this quiet space, where no one's sane.

Whispers linger like candy floss,
Tickling silently, never a loss.
They skate on the surface, just for a jest,
A chuckle here, a whisper blessed.

Each soft echo has a quirky tale,
Of misadventures that never pale.
Like cats in hats tossing around,
In the weight of laughter, we all are bound.

So listen closely to the giggling sound,
In the hush of echoes, joy is found.
The weight of soft laughter is a treasure dear,
In this merry world, hold it near!

Milton Keynes UK
Ingram Content Group UK Ltd.
UKHW021242191124
451300UK00007B/200